Ellen Oc

CHERRY LAKE PRESS

Published in the United States of America by Cherry Lake Publishing
Ann Arbor, Michigan
www.cherrylakepublishing.com

Reading Adviser: Beth Walker Gambro, MS, Ed., Reading Consultant, Yorkville, IL
Illustrator: Leo Trinidad

Photo Credits: Adoramassey via Wikimedia Commons CC BY SA 4.0, 5; © Shaiith / Shutterstock, 7; Courtesy of NASA, 9, 17; NASA on The Commons / Flickr Commons, 11, 22; NASA APPEL Knowledge Services, 13; NASA Johnson Space Center, 15; © ASSOCIATED PRESS, 19, 21, 23

Cherry Lake Press is an imprint of Cherry Lake Publishing Group

Library of Congress Cataloging-in-Publication Data has been filed and is available at catalog.loc.gov.

Printed in the United States of America

About the author: Brenda Perez Mendoza is an award-winning educator and the author of the Racial Justice in America: Latinx American series. She grew up in Cicero, Illinois, as a native language Spanish speaker. When she went to school, there wasn't enough support for students learning the English language. That is what drove her to become a K–12 ELL specialist and work with bilingual students. She works to advocate for all students, Latinx especially, to embrace their culture and celebrate who they are. Today, she lives in Chicago, Illinois, and is committed to providing students with culturally responsive practices and advocating for the whole child.

About the illustrator: Leo Trinidad is a NY Times bestselling comic book artist, illustrator, and animator from Costa Rica. For more than 12 years he's been creating content for children's books and TV shows. Leo created the first animated series ever produced in Central America, and founded Rocket Cartoons, one of the most successful animation studios in Latin America. He is also the 2018 winner of the Central American Graphic Novel contest.

I was born in Los Angeles, California, in 1958. I have four siblings.

My grandparents were Mexican **immigrants**.

I went to college. I studied science. I worked hard.

I got a **doctorate**.

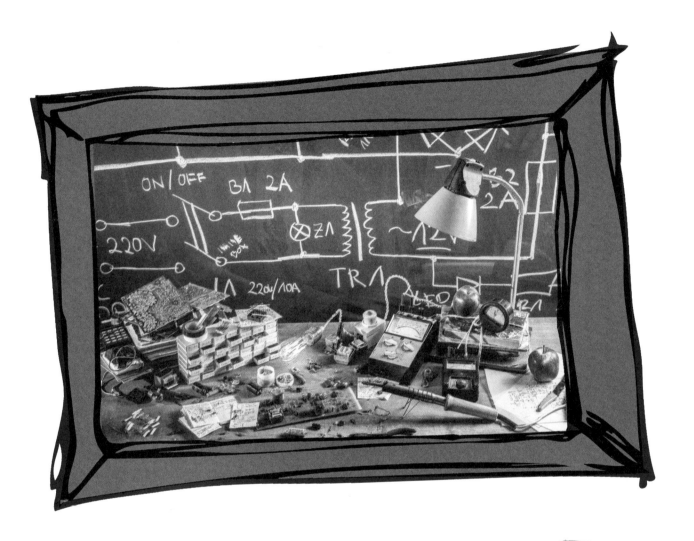

What do you like to learn about?

I became an **engineer**. I worked at **NASA**.

Then I became an astronaut.

I was the first Latina in space! That was in 1993. I was in space for 9 days.

I played my flute in space.

What would you do in space?

I went to space three more times. I was in space almost 1,000 hours!

I was on the International Space Station.

Later, I worked at the Johnson Space Center.

I was its **director**.

I received the Distinguished Service Medal. That is NASA's biggest honor. I got it in 2015.

I retired from NASA in 2018.

I visit schools. I give talks. I tell people how important science is. I tell them how important teamwork is.

I tell Hispanic students to reach for the stars.

I received the Presidential Medal of Freedom. I got it in 2024. I thanked the people who worked with me.

I did not do it alone.

What would you like to ask me?

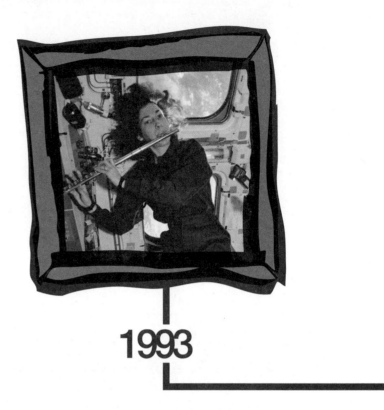

1993

1930

Born
1958

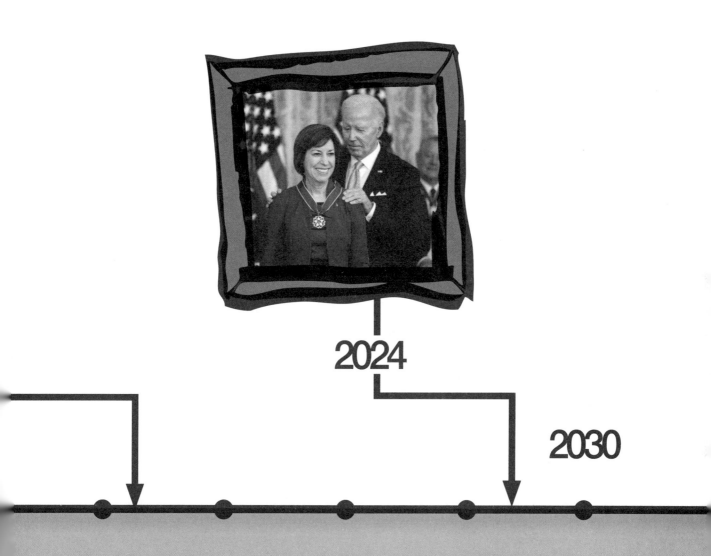

2024

2030

glossary

director (duh-REK-ter) a person in charge of an organization or group

doctorate (DAHK-tuh-ruht) the highest educational degree

engineer (en-juh-NEER) a person who designs, builds, or fixes machines or engines

immigrants (IH-muh-gruhnts) people who move to one country from another country

NASA (NAA-suh) stands for National Aeronautics and Space Administration, the U.S. government agency that explores space

index